PADP

Source of Creativity

Ideas for Art & Illustration

PADP offers phantastic art & design posters as a source of ideas for your own art projects. PADP's extensive art archive includes collections of historical images, prints & motif templates dating 15th - 20th century. Many of those images and drawings are comparable to master illustrations in today's media design. Sourcing from this pool the current poster set was created. The originals can usually only be admired in a variety of scattered sources or in the libraries of private collectors.

The 1920s Fashion |01|» 22 Poster

The 22 art prints reflect diverse approaches to design, art & illustration. Art ideas and abstract paths become comprehensible through original work samples, which offer new visual approaches for art classes, graphics or DIY projects. Whether picture or sketch, the pattern icons of art are still breathtaking in illustration & design.

Poster: padp.art/03/the-1920s-fashion-01-poster-22-isbn-9783987840005.jpg

Poster - Images: The 1920s Fashion |01|» 22 Poster

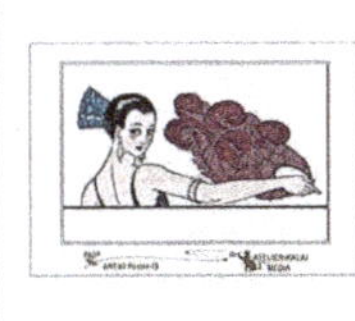

Poster-Set: padp.art/03/the-1920s-fashion-01-poster-set-isbn-9783987840005.jpg

The 1920s Fashion |01|» 22 Poster
is the english version of the german title
„Goldene Zwanziger |01|» Modedesign"

PADP
Source of Creativity

Publisher / Editorial Office
Picture editing and artistic design
of the posters, image templates & drawings by

ATELIER•KALAI•MEDIA
Kerstin Winter, Kirchengasse 12, 91245 Simmelsdorf / Germany

Copyright Note

Title-Information about the "First english Issue"

Product-ID	padp-art-03
Execution:	Posterbook Paperback, 22 Art Prints A4 color printed on 70lb white paper.
Product group:	padp.art
Category:	padp.style
Collection:	padp-style-fashion-design
Series title & No.:	The 1920s Fashion | 01
Content:	Framable Pictures | Images | 22 Poster » Roaring 20s Fashion » Fashion Design
Images:	padp.art/03/the-1920s-fashion-01-poster-set-isbn-9783987840005.jpg
Keywords & Tags:	Poster Book, Fashion Magazine, Fashion Drawing, Fashion Sketches, Fashion Designs, Framable Pictures, Office Poster
Publisher's Programme:	padp-art.info/poster-catalogue-2022-05.pdf

Note:
"First Issue" indicates the first edition of a product ID in the respective language.

ATELIER•KALAI•MEDIA
1. Edition 2022
ISBN: 9783987840005

PADP

ART-03 Poster 01

ATELIER·KALAI
MEDIA

PADP
ART-03 Poster 02

ATELIER·KALAI
MEDIA

PADP
ART-03 Poster 03
ATELIER·KALAI
MEDIA

PADP
ART-03 Poster 04

ATELIER•KALAI
MEDIA

PADP

ART-03 Poster 05

ATELIER•KALAI
MEDIA

PADP
ART-03 Poster 06

ATELIER·KALAI
MEDIA

PADP
ART-03 Poster 07
ATELIER·KALAI
MEDIA

PADP

ART-03 Poster 09

ATELIER·KALAI
MEDIA

PADP

ART-03 Poster 10

PADP
ART-03 Poster 11
ATELIER·KALAI
MEDIA

PADP
ART-03 Poster 12

ATELIER·KALAI
MEDIA

PADP

ART-03 Poster 13

PADP
ART-03 Poster 14

ATELIER·KALAI
MEDIA

PADP
ART-03 Poster 15

ATELIER•KALAI
MEDIA

ATELIER·KALAI
MEDIA

ATELIER·KALAI
MEDIA

PADP
ART-03 Poster 18
ATELIER·KALAI
MEDIA

ATELIER·KALAI
MEDIA

PADP
ART-03 Poster-19

PADP

ART-03 Poster 20

PADP

ART-03 Poster 21

PADP
ART-03 Poster 22
ATELIER·KALAI
MEDIA

PADP

Partner der Phantasie

Buchstaben sticken

Stickmuster Vorlagen für Namen Initialen Monogramm
Anfangsbuchstaben, ABC, Schrift und Alphabet

Stickvorlage selbst zeichnen, selber sticken und
besticken, Modedesign, Textiles Gestalten von
Hand, Handarbeiten, Textildesign, Graphikdesign

ATELIER KALAI

PADP 01 SCRIPT — PUBLIC ART & DESIGN PROJECT

Buchstaben sticken II

Schreibschrift bis Jugendstil, Kreuzstich Vorlagen zum nähen,
malen & zeichnen, stempeln & drucken, seidenmalerei & quilling.

Dekor, Grafik, Mode, Design, Modeschneider
Seidenmalerei, Applikation, Handarbeiten,
Quilling Schablonen aus Pappe selber machen.

ATELIER KALAI

PADP 02 SCRIPT — PUBLIC ART & DESIGN PROJECT

Schriften im Mittelalter

Schriftarten von 700 bis 1500 A.D.
Vorlagen zum Malen, Zeichnen, Besticken und Stempeln.

Buchstaben Muster für Urkunden, Kalligraphie,
Seidenmalerei, Graffiti, Tattoo und Stempel
Mode - Textildesign, Grafikdesign Schmuckdesign

ATELIER KALAI

PADP 03 SCRIPT — PUBLIC ART & DESIGN PROJECT

Schriften der Neuzeit

Alte Schriftarten / Schriftmuster von Johannes Gutenberg
über Albrecht Dürer bis in die französische Revolution 1789.

Buchstaben Muster für Urkunden, Tattoo, Graffiti,
Stempel und Druck. Seidenmalerei, Zeichnen, Malen
und Besticken. Mode - Textil-, Grafik- Schmuckdesign

ATELIER KALAI

PADP 04 SCRIPT — PUBLIC ART & DESIGN PROJECT

Kalligraphie & Mandala

Monogramm, Initiale, Anfangsbuchstabe, Namenszeichen,
Signet, verschnörkelte Schrift-Vorlagen festlich verziert.

Buchstaben Muster für Urkunden, Tattoo, Kalligraphie,
Seidenmalerei, Versalien Zeichnen, Malen und Besticken
Mode - Textildesign, Grafikdesign Schmuckdesign

ATELIER KALAI

PADP 05 SCRIPT — PUBLIC ART & DESIGN PROJECT

Musterbuch I

Stricken, weben, knüpfen, häkeln, sticken
geometrische Vorlagen für Pullover & Decke · 1771

Leinen und Bildweberkunst
Handarbeiten, Strickmuster, Patchwork, Muster
Wolle - Textildesign, Grafikdesign, Modedesign

ATELIER KALAI

PADP 06 SCRIPT — PUBLIC ART & DESIGN PROJECT

Musterbuch II

Strickmuster, Webmuster, Häkelmuster für
Webrahmen, Topflappen, Schal u. Poncho · 1771

Leinen und Bildweberkunst, Armbänder knüpfen
Muster, Vorlagen. Freundschaftsbänder selbst geknüpft.
Stoffmuster, Entwürfe für Möbelstoffe, Polsterstoffe, Teppich

ATELIER KALAI

PADP 07 SCRIPT — PUBLIC ART & DESIGN PROJECT

Venezianische Spitze 1591

No 1: LOCHSPITZE u. RICHELIEUSTICKEREI
Designerspitze, Vorlagen, Muster, Motive

Handarbeiten, Strickmuster, vintage Lace Stickerei
Dirndl, Kleid, Brautkleid, Hochzeitskleid, Maske
Wolle - Textildesign, Grafikdesign, Modedesign

ATELIER KALAI

PADP 08 SCRIPT — PUBLIC ART & DESIGN PROJECT

Venezianische Spitze 1591

No 2: STICKMUSTER und DESIGNVORLAGEN
Sticken, Häkeln, Stricken, Weben, Klöppeln

Handarbeiten, Strickmuster, vintage Lace Stickerei
Dirndl, Kleid, Brautkleid, Hochzeitskleid, Maske
Wolle - Textildesign, Grafikdesign, Modedesign

ATELIER KALAI

PADP 09 SCRIPT — PUBLIC ART & DESIGN PROJECT

Blumen sticken - Doodle Stitching

oder wie Sticken Schritt für Schritt zur Passion wird!
Ideenbuch der Stickerei. Stickmuster und Stickvorlagen
für alle Techniken der Nutz- und Zierstiche von 1619 AD.

Dirndl, Trachten, Lederhose und Handschuhe mit Weiß-
und Goldstickerei. Kissen, Borten und Bordüren sticken
Kleider und Dessous, Hauben und Mieder selber besticken

ATELIER KALAI

PADP 10 SCRIPT — PUBLIC ART & DESIGN PROJECT

Kalligraphie lernen

Vorlagen - Übungen - Zeichentechniken, Tusche -
Zeichnung & Zeichnungen mit Bleistift für Anfänger

Arbeitsbuch - Malvorlagen, Bilder & Motive
Rasterzeichnung Vorlagen zum Zeichnen mit Raster
Kalligraphie Buch II

ATELIER KALAI

PADP 11 SCRIPT — PUBLIC ART & DESIGN PROJECT